The Paper Propeller
The Spinning Quarter
The Jumping Frog

+ 38 OTHER AMAZING TRICKS YOU CAN DO WITH STUFF LYING AROUND THE HOUSE

Arthur Okamura

Shelter Publications
Bolinas, California

DISTRIBUTED IN THE UNITED STATES AND CANADA BY PUBLISHERS GROUP WEST, BERKELEY, CALIFORNIA

LIBRARY OF CONGRESS
CATALOGING-IN-PUBLICATION DATA

OKAMURA, ARTHUR.
    THE PAPER PROPELLER, THE JUMPING FROG, THE SPINNING QUARTER : + 38 AMAZING
TRICKS YOU CAN DO WITH STUFF LYING AROUND THE HOUSE / ARTHUR OKAMURA.
    P.   CM.
INCLUDES BIBLIOGRAPHICAL REFERENCES AND INDEX.
ISBN 0-936070-23-4 (PBK. : ALK. PAPER)
1. TRICKS — JUVENILE LITERATURE.   1. TITLE.

GV1548.043 2000
793.8 — DC21   00-063572

FIRST AMERICAN PRINTING 2000
8 7 6 5 4 3 — 05 04 03 02 01 00
(LOWEST DIGITS INDICATE NUMBER AND YEAR OF LATEST PRINTING)

ADDITIONAL COPIES OF THIS BOOK MAY BE PURCHASED AT YOUR LOCAL BOOKSTORE,
BY CALLING US AT 1-800-307-0131, OR ON OUR WEBSITE (SEE BELOW):

SHELTER PUBLICATIONS, INC.
P. O. BOX 279
BOLINAS, CALIFORNIA 94924 USA
WWW.SHELTERPUB.COM

Introduction

THESE ARE SOME OF MY FAVORITE TRICKS, SOME LEARNED AS A KID, AND OTHERS, THROUGH THE YEARS, FROM MANY PEOPLE IN MANY PLACES AND COUNTRIES.

MOST OF THE TRICKS REQUIRE THE SIMPLEST OF MATERIALS AND THINGS THAT ARE COMMONLY AT HAND. UNLIKE "MAGIC TRICKS," THEY DO NOT REQUIRE DECEPTION. NOR IS THERE ANY NEED TO KEEP THEM SECRET. THEY CAN BE SHOWN AND SHARED WITH OTHERS, AND PASSED ON, AS THEY WERE TO ME.

EVERYWHERE YOU DO THESE — AROUND A TABLE WITH FRIENDS, AT PARTIES, IN A RESTAURANT — THEY WILL CREATE SURPRISE, RESPONSE, AND PARTICIPATION FROM ANYONE WATCHING. PEOPLE ARE INTRIGUED AND OFTEN AMAZED AT THE RESULTS.

ONE THING: SOME OF THE TRICKS ARE HARDER TO MASTER THAN OTHERS. SOME YOU MIGHT HAVE TO WORK AT (ESPECIALLY THOSE REQUIRING MANUAL DEXTERITY); OTHERS YOU'LL BE ABLE TO DO RIGHT OFF THE BAT.

I FIND THEM TO BE ESPECIALLY WONDERFUL WHEN TRAVELLING. THEY SEEM TO AMUSE AND DELIGHT EVERYONE, ELIMINATING ANY LANGUAGE, AGE, OR CULTURAL DIFFERENCES. (THAT'S WHY WE MADE THE BOOK SO IT WILL FIT IN YOUR POCKET.)

HAVE FUN!

ARTHUR

Contents

A Pre-Sliced Banana

OFFER A BANANA TO A FRIEND,
AND WATCH HIS AMAZEMENT,
AS HE UNPEELS A PRE-SLICED BANANA

HOW TO SLICE A BANANA
WITHOUT ANYONE KNOWING

WITH A LONG SEWING NEEDLE,
PUNCTURE THRU THE PEEL
ALONG A SEAM & USE SIDEWAY
CIRCULAR MOTIONS TO CREATE
SEGMENTS. SMOOTH OVER
PUNCTURE MARKS WITH FINGERS.

The Fork & Spoon Fulcrum

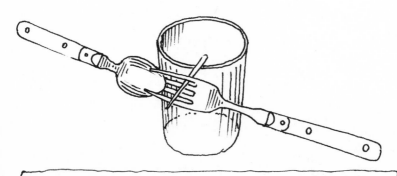

FIT FORK & SPOON TOGETHER AS SHOWN. FIND CENTER OF BALANCE UNDER FIRST TINE OF FORK WITH A FLAT TOOTHPICK OR MATCHSTICK.

PLACE THE ASSEMBLY ON THE EDGE OF A GLASS AND IT WILL BALANCE.

IF BLOWN SOFTLY IT WILL SLOWLY MOVE WHILE MAINTAINING ITS BALANCE.

The Extended Knife Platform

CAN YOU BALANCE THE COFFEE CUP AT THE SAME HEIGHT AS THE 3 GLASSES, USING THE 3 KNIVES? NOTICE THAT THE DISTANCE BETWEEN THE GLASSES IS GREATER THAN THE LENGTH OF THE KNIVES.

ANSWER: NEXT PAGE

WEAVE THE KNIVES TOGETHER
AS SHOWN. NOTICE HOW THEY SPAN
THE DISTANCE BETWEEN THE GLASSES.
NOW SIMPLY PUT THE COFFEE CUP
ON THE CENTER PLATFORM.

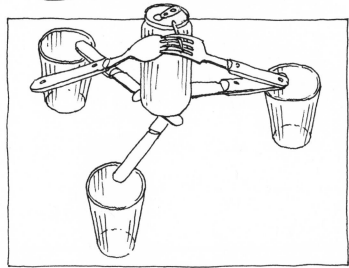

P.S. FLAT TOOTHPICKS PROVIDE THE BEST FINE EDGE FOR THE FULCRUM TO BALANCE & ROTATE.

YOU CAN TRY MANY COMBINATIONS OF OBJECTS.

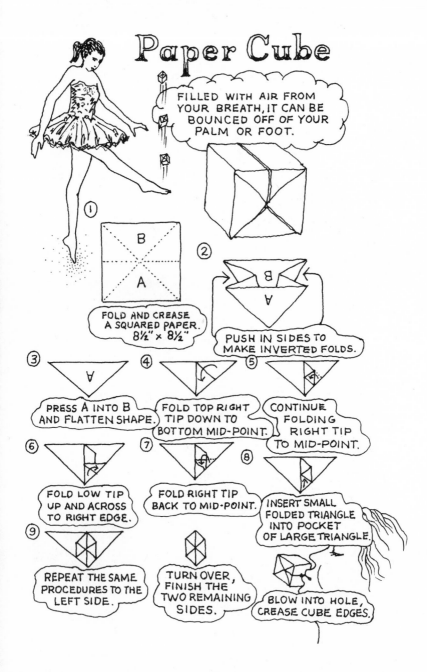

Paper Cube

FILLED WITH AIR FROM YOUR BREATH, IT CAN BE BOUNCED OFF OF YOUR PALM OR FOOT.

① B A

FOLD AND CREASE A SQUARED PAPER. 8½" × 8½"

② B A

PUSH IN SIDES TO MAKE INVERTED FOLDS.

③ A

PRESS A INTO B AND FLATTEN SHAPE.

④ FOLD TOP RIGHT TIP DOWN TO BOTTOM MID-POINT.

⑤ CONTINUE FOLDING RIGHT TIP TO MID-POINT.

⑥ FOLD LOW TIP UP AND ACROSS TO RIGHT EDGE.

⑦ FOLD RIGHT TIP BACK TO MID-POINT.

⑧ INSERT SMALL FOLDED TRIANGLE INTO POCKET OF LARGE TRIANGLE.

⑨ REPEAT THE SAME PROCEDURES TO THE LEFT SIDE.

TURN OVER, FINISH THE TWO REMAINING SIDES.

BLOW INTO HOLE, CREASE CUBE EDGES.

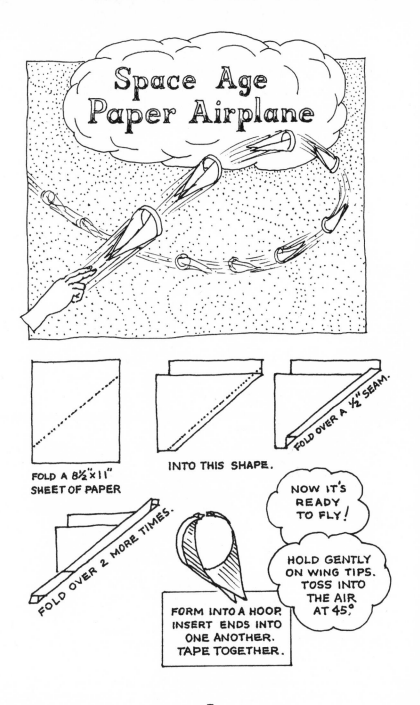

Space Age Paper Airplane

FOLD A 8½"×11" SHEET OF PAPER

INTO THIS SHAPE.

FOLD OVER A ½" SEAM.

FOLD OVER 2 MORE TIMES.

FORM INTO A HOOP. INSERT ENDS INTO ONE ANOTHER. TAPE TOGETHER.

NOW IT'S READY TO FLY!

HOLD GENTLY ON WING TIPS. TOSS INTO THE AIR AT 45°.

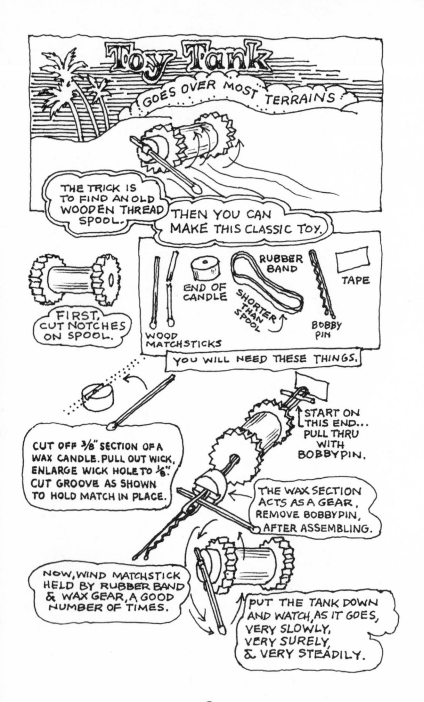

Toy Tank

GOES OVER MOST TERRAINS

THE TRICK IS TO FIND AN OLD WOODEN THREAD SPOOL.

THEN YOU CAN MAKE THIS CLASSIC TOY.

FIRST, CUT NOTCHES ON SPOOL.

RUBBER BAND

END OF CANDLE

SHORTER THAN SPOOL

TAPE

BOBBY PIN

WOOD MATCHSTICKS

YOU WILL NEED THESE THINGS.

CUT OFF ³⁄₈" SECTION OF A WAX CANDLE. PULL OUT WICK, ENLARGE WICK HOLE TO ⅛" CUT GROOVE AS SHOWN TO HOLD MATCH IN PLACE.

START ON THIS END... PULL THRU WITH BOBBYPIN.

THE WAX SECTION ACTS AS A GEAR, REMOVE BOBBYPIN, AFTER ASSEMBLING.

NOW, WIND MATCHSTICK HELD BY RUBBER BAND & WAX GEAR, A GOOD NUMBER OF TIMES.

PUT THE TANK DOWN AND WATCH, AS IT GOES, VERY SLOWLY, VERY SURELY, & VERY STEADILY.

8

Draw A Star In A Mirror

TRY TO DRAW A STAR BETWEEN TWO OTHER STARS WHILE LOOKING AT THE IMAGE REFLECTED IN A MIRROR. HOLD A SHEET OF PAPER IN FRONT OF EYES AND THE DRAWING OF STARS.

LOOK ONLY AT THE MIRROR REFLECTION.

A REAL BRAIN TWISTER!

9

Ink Blot Signature

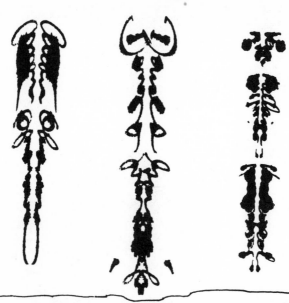

THESE ARE SIGNATURES MADE BY BLOTTING.

TRY YOUR OWN, BY USING A PEN POINT DIPPED WITH INK. USE SMOOTH NON-ABSORBENT PAPER. TRACING PAPER WORKS WELL.

MAKE A CREASE. SIGN NAME ON TOP HALF.

REFOLD TO BLOT, THEN UNFOLD. WOW!

A Paper Net

START WITH A SQUARE 8"× 8" PAPER

FOLD INTO TRIANGULAR HALVES, AS SHOWN.

CUT OFF END

MAKE ALTERNATE CUTS AS SHOWN

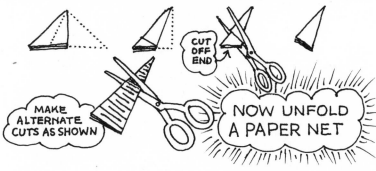

NOW UNFOLD A PAPER NET

A One-Cut Star

MEASURE OUT A 8¾" x 6¼" PIECE OF PAPER. FOLD IN HALF.

FOLD TO CORNER

FROM CENTER POINT...

FOLD LEFT HALF SIMILARLY.

FOLD RIGHT SECTION OVER MIDDLE AREA

FOLD OVER ONCE AGAIN TO EDGE

CUT TO OVERLAPPED FOLD CORNER.

NOW UNFOLD A PERFECT FIVE-POINTED STAR!

The Spinning Thumbtacks

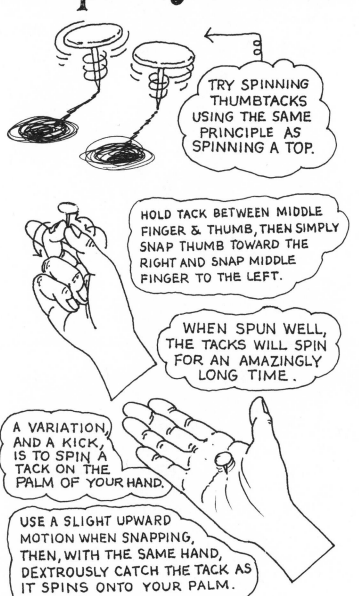

TRY SPINNING THUMBTACKS USING THE SAME PRINCIPLE AS SPINNING A TOP.

HOLD TACK BETWEEN MIDDLE FINGER & THUMB, THEN SIMPLY SNAP THUMB TOWARD THE RIGHT AND SNAP MIDDLE FINGER TO THE LEFT.

WHEN SPUN WELL, THE TACKS WILL SPIN FOR AN AMAZINGLY LONG TIME.

A VARIATION, AND A KICK, IS TO SPIN A TACK ON THE PALM OF YOUR HAND.

USE A SLIGHT UPWARD MOTION WHEN SNAPPING, THEN, WITH THE SAME HAND, DEXTROUSLY CATCH THE TACK AS IT SPINS ONTO YOUR PALM.

The Jumping Match

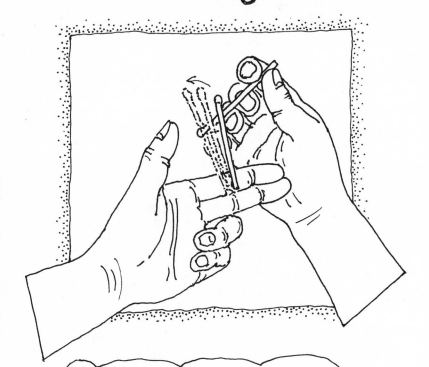

HOLD A WOOD MATCH BETWEEN
THUMB & FOREFINGER WHILE
APPLYING STRONG PRESSURE
AGAINST THE MIDDLE FINGERNAIL.
BALANCE ANOTHER MATCH ON
TOP AND IT WILL MYSTERIOUSLY
POP UP & DOWN.

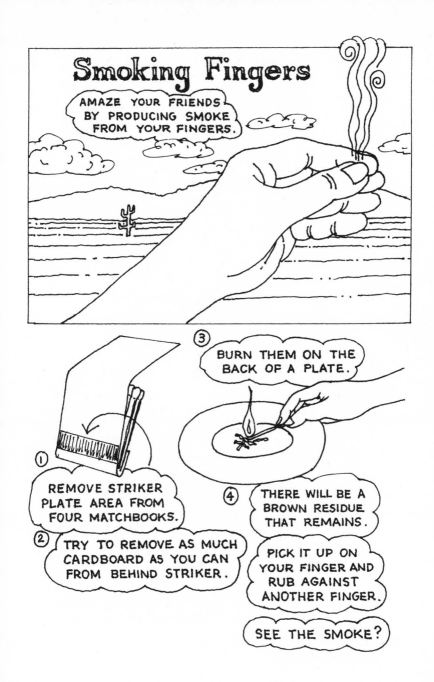

Burnt Match On Ceiling

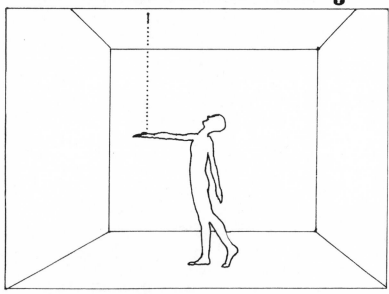

MAKE IT STICK ON CEILING

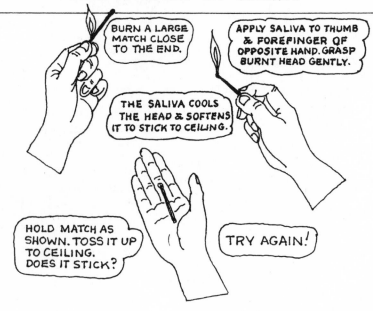

BURN A LARGE MATCH CLOSE TO THE END.

APPLY SALIVA TO THUMB & FOREFINGER OF OPPOSITE HAND. GRASP BURNT HEAD GENTLY.

THE SALIVA COOLS THE HEAD & SOFTENS IT TO STICK TO CEILING.

HOLD MATCH AS SHOWN. TOSS IT UP TO CEILING. DOES IT STICK?

TRY AGAIN!

Clothes Pin Gun

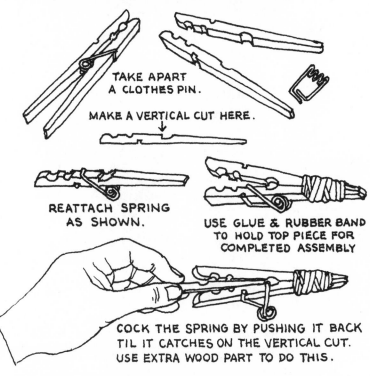

TAKE APART
A CLOTHES PIN.

MAKE A VERTICAL CUT HERE.

REATTACH SPRING
AS SHOWN.

USE GLUE & RUBBER BAND
TO HOLD TOP PIECE FOR
COMPLETED ASSEMBLY

COCK THE SPRING BY PUSHING IT BACK
TIL IT CATCHES ON THE VERTICAL CUT.
USE EXTRA WOOD PART TO DO THIS.

INSERT A *PRE-BURNED WOOD MATCH INTO
THE SLOT. NOW IT'S READY TO SHOOT.
*FOR SAFETY.

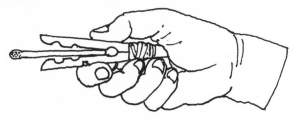

AIM CAREFULLY, THEN PULL TRIGGER.
SCHPLAT!

Reverse Sweater To Inside/Out With Hands Tied

WEAR A PULLOVER SWEATER.
TIE EACH HAND WITH A LENGTH
OF STRING ABOUT 30" LONG

REMOVE SWEATER...
IT WILL BE INSIDE OUT.

NOW CAN YOU
PUT THE SWEATER
BACK ON, WITH THE
INSIDE—OUT?

SOLUTION:

PULL SLEEVE OF ONE ARM OUT THRU
THE OTHER SLEEVE & CONTINUE TO PULL THRU
THE ENTIRE SWEATER. NOW, PUT ARMS, STILL
TIED, THRU THE SLEEVES, SLIP HEAD THRU
OPENING & PULL SWEATER OVER TORSO.

A Chair, A Woman & A Man

The Jumping Frog

FOLD A 3"x 6" PAPER INTO THESE CREASES.

PUSH INTO THIS SHAPE.

DOUBLE FOLDING IN BOTH DIRECTIONS MAKES IT EASIER.

PUSH THE FOLDS TOGETHER AS SHOWN.

TURN OVER. FLATTEN INTO SQUARE SHAPE.

FOLD RIGHT CORNER TO MIDDLE.

FOLD LEFT CORNER TO MIDDLE.

FOLD UP HERE.

INSERT RIGHT TRIANGLE INTO POCKET OF FOLDED-UP TRIANGLE.

INSERT LEFT TRIANGLE.

20

TURN OVER.

FOLD DOWN BACK LEG HERE.

THEN FOLD THE OTHER SIDE TO COMPLETE LEGS.

TURN OVER. MAKE A ¼" FOLD HERE.

MAKE ANOTHER ¼" FOLD TO CREATE AN ACCORDION FOLD THAT WILL POWER THE JUMP.

TURN OVER. FOLD UP RIGHT SIDE TO TOP POINT.

THEN THE LEFT SIDE TO COMPLETE THE FRONT LEGS.

TURN OVER. DRAW IN THE EYES, NOW IT'S READY TO JUMP.

HOLD DOWN & PULL BACK THE FOLD TO COMPRESS & THEN TO POWER THE JUMP.

SNAP FINGER BACK AND WATCH IT JUMP.

ALL RIGHT!

Two Guys Die & Go To Heaven

FIRST, FOR THIS TRICK AND STORY, YOU MUST MAKE A PASSPORT.

FOLD A RECTANGLE

LIKE THIS

HI GUYS, WELCOME TO HEAVEN

GIVE ME YOUR PASSPORTS

HEAVEN

HERE'S MY PASSPORT!

THEY DIDN'T TELL ME I NEEDED A PASSPORT TO GET INTO HEAVEN.

MAYBE HE'LL LET YOU IN WITH A PART OF MINE.

HE MAKES THIS CUT.

⅓ OF WIDTH
4 PIECES FALL

ST. PETER UNFOLDS THE PIECES AND SAYS...

THIS IS NOT GOING TO GET YOU INTO HEAVEN.

23

Pick up 3 matches with ONE match

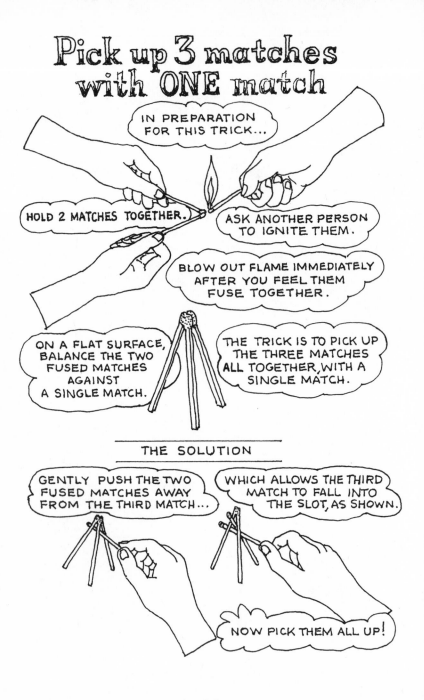

IN PREPARATION FOR THIS TRICK...

HOLD 2 MATCHES TOGETHER.

ASK ANOTHER PERSON TO IGNITE THEM.

BLOW OUT FLAME IMMEDIATELY AFTER YOU FEEL THEM FUSE TOGETHER.

ON A FLAT SURFACE, BALANCE THE TWO FUSED MATCHES AGAINST A SINGLE MATCH.

THE TRICK IS TO PICK UP THE THREE MATCHES ALL TOGETHER, WITH A SINGLE MATCH.

THE SOLUTION

GENTLY PUSH THE TWO FUSED MATCHES AWAY FROM THE THIRD MATCH...

WHICH ALLOWS THE THIRD MATCH TO FALL INTO THE SLOT, AS SHOWN.

NOW PICK THEM ALL UP!

The Spinning Clotheshanger & Penny

SPIN A PENNY AS IT BALANCES ON THE HOOK OF A WIRE HANGER. USE A HEAVY-GAUGE HANGER.

PULL HANGER INTO THIS ELONGATED SHAPE. FILE END OF HOOK FLAT.

THE PENNY WILL REMAIN IN PLACE DURING SPIN. MAINTAIN AN EVEN SPIN, NOT TOO FAST, NOT TOO SLOW.

BALANCE PENNY TAIL SIDE DOWN ON HOOK.

USE THUMB TO FEEL THE CENTER POINT OF BALANCE...

...THE FIRST TWO FINGERS UNDERNEATH, TO SUPPORT THE PENNY.

Lew's Big Bubbles

HOW TO BLOW BUBBLES BY SIMPLY
USING YOUR HANDS & DISH SOAP.

WASH YOUR HANDS
THOROUGHLY TO REMOVE
ANY IMPURITIES.

NOW, MIX A SMALL AMOUNT
OF SOAP & WATER IN YOUR
HANDS TO MAKE BUBBLES...
JUST A SQUEEZE OR TWO
& A FEW DROPS OF WATER.

MAKE AN OPENING WITH BACK
SIDE OF PALMS, AND, AT THE
SAME TIME, CREATE A FILM OF
SOAP THAT STRETCHES ACROSS
THE OPENING. YOU WILL SEE
SMALL BUBBLES & A SHEEN
STRETCHING ACROSS OPENING.

BLOW INTO PALMS AT THE
FILM OF SOAP. CAN YOU BLOW
A BUBBLE? TO GET ONE IN
THE AIR, STEP BACK AND
CLOSE OPENING, AS YOU BLOW. GOT ONE?

Cutting A Mobius Strip Into Halves

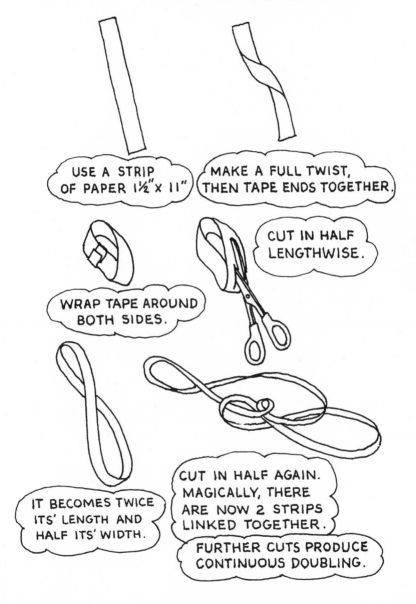

USE A STRIP OF PAPER 1½" x 11"

MAKE A FULL TWIST, THEN TAPE ENDS TOGETHER.

WRAP TAPE AROUND BOTH SIDES.

CUT IN HALF LENGTHWISE.

IT BECOMES TWICE ITS' LENGTH AND HALF ITS' WIDTH.

CUT IN HALF AGAIN. MAGICALLY, THERE ARE NOW 2 STRIPS LINKED TOGETHER.

FURTHER CUTS PRODUCE CONTINUOUS DOUBLING.

Nail Fulcrum

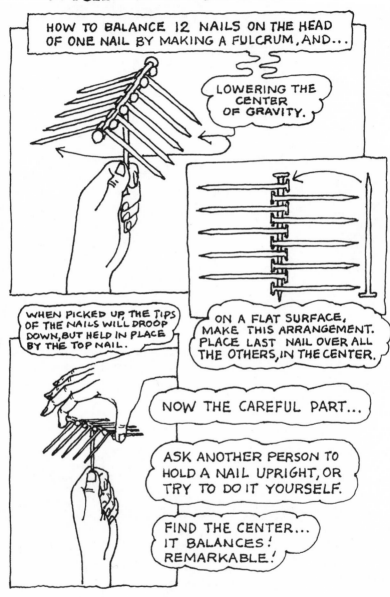

HOW TO BALANCE 12 NAILS ON THE HEAD OF ONE NAIL BY MAKING A FULCRUM, AND...

LOWERING THE CENTER OF GRAVITY.

ON A FLAT SURFACE, MAKE THIS ARRANGEMENT. PLACE LAST NAIL OVER ALL THE OTHERS, IN THE CENTER.

WHEN PICKED UP, THE TIPS OF THE NAILS WILL DROOP DOWN, BUT HELD IN PLACE BY THE TOP NAIL.

NOW THE CAREFUL PART...

ASK ANOTHER PERSON TO HOLD A NAIL UPRIGHT, OR TRY TO DO IT YOURSELF.

FIND THE CENTER... IT BALANCES! REMARKABLE!

The Small To Big Cut

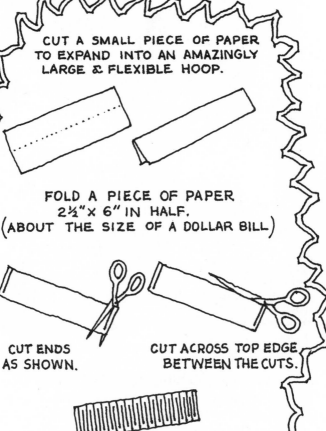

CUT A SMALL PIECE OF PAPER
TO EXPAND INTO AN AMAZINGLY
LARGE & FLEXIBLE HOOP.

FOLD A PIECE OF PAPER
2½" x 6" IN HALF.
(ABOUT THE SIZE OF A DOLLAR BILL)

CUT ENDS
AS SHOWN.

CUT ACROSS TOP EDGE
BETWEEN THE CUTS.

HOLD CAREFULLY WHILE MAKING
ALTERNATE CUTS ⅛" APART
AS SHOWN. WHEN FINISHED,
UNFOLD. WOW!

The Paper Propeller

SPIN A PAPER PROPELLER ON YOUR FINGERTIP.

IT'S A DELIGHT!

FOLD A CIGARETTE ROLLING PAPER INTO THIS BOX-LIKE SHAPE. PINCH CORNERS FOR SHAPE.

PLACE TIP OF FOREFINGER AT EXACT CENTER THEN HOLD IN PLACE WITH THUMB. FACE BOX OPENING FORWARD.

NOW THE FUN PART. FULLY EXTEND ARM AND BEND WRIST & FOREFINGER INTO THE DIRECTION OF YOUR TURNING BODY.

AFTER YOU GET GOING, REMOVE THUMB. THE PROPELLER WILL SPIN.

Toothpick Star

FRACTURE TOOTHPICKS AS SHOWN.

USE END OF FOREFINGER. PLACE A SINGLE DROP OF WATER ON EXACT CENTER POINT OF ARRANGEMENT.

THE WATER WILL EXPAND THE WOOD, AND VERY SLOWLY, A STAR WILL BEGIN TO EMERGE AND EXPAND OUTWARD.

DO THIS ON A SMOOTH SURFACE, SUCH AS, THE BACK OF A FLAT DISH.

Recycling An Aluminum Can

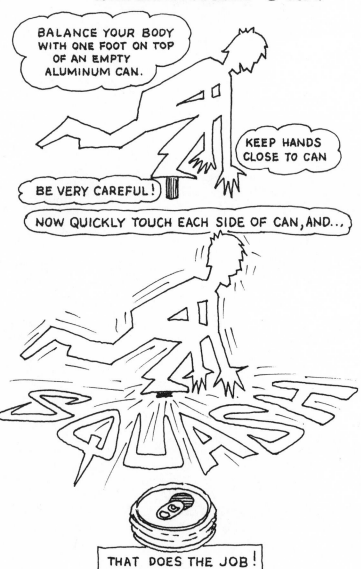

Paper Rabbit

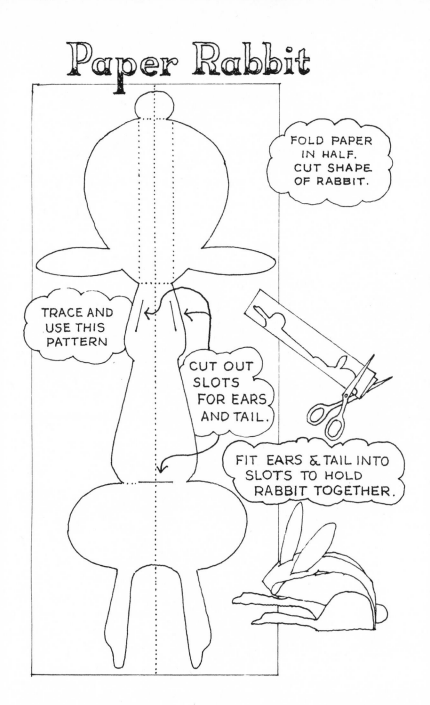

FOLD PAPER IN HALF. CUT SHAPE OF RABBIT.

TRACE AND USE THIS PATTERN

CUT OUT SLOTS FOR EARS AND TAIL.

FIT EARS & TAIL INTO SLOTS TO HOLD RABBIT TOGETHER.

Untying A Knot In A Hair

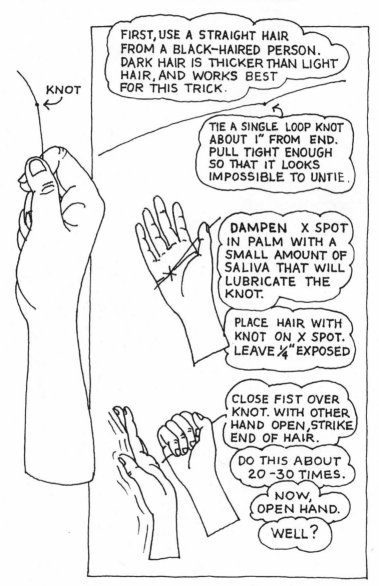

KNOT

FIRST, USE A STRAIGHT HAIR FROM A BLACK-HAIRED PERSON. DARK HAIR IS THICKER THAN LIGHT HAIR, AND WORKS BEST FOR THIS TRICK.

TIE A SINGLE LOOP KNOT ABOUT 1" FROM END. PULL TIGHT ENOUGH SO THAT IT LOOKS IMPOSSIBLE TO UNTIE.

DAMPEN X SPOT IN PALM WITH A SMALL AMOUNT OF SALIVA THAT WILL LUBRICATE THE KNOT.

PLACE HAIR WITH KNOT ON X SPOT. LEAVE ¼" EXPOSED

CLOSE FIST OVER KNOT. WITH OTHER HAND OPEN, STRIKE END OF HAIR.

DO THIS ABOUT 20-30 TIMES.

NOW, OPEN HAND.

WELL?

The Spinning Quarter

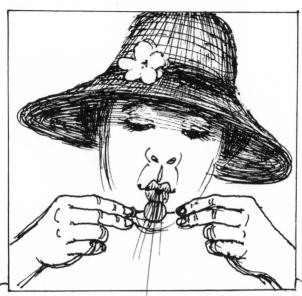

BLOW AT, AND SPIN, A QUARTER AT
HIGH RPMs. IT WILL ALSO MAKE
A VERY PLEASANT WHIRRING SOUND.

PICK UP A QUARTER AT THE CENTER
AXIS USING TWO PUSH PINS.
THE SERRATED EDGES WILL
PROVIDE GROOVES TO HOLD
THE POINTS IN PLACE.

Open A Bottle
With A Quarter

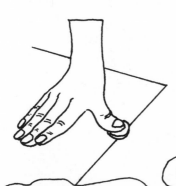

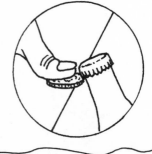

ASK A FRIEND TO HOLD DOWN A QUARTER ON A FLAT LEDGE. LEAVE ⅛" OVERHANG.

HOLD BOTTLE AND PLACE SERRATED EDGE OF CAP OVER LIP OF QUARTER.

WITH A CLOSED FIST, SMARTLY STRIKE THE TOP OF THE CAP.

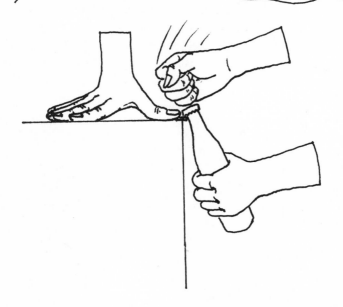

Paper Paradox

The Paper Tree

ROLL 6 FULL SHEETS OF NEWSPAPER, END TO END, INTO A COMPACT TUBE.

WITH SCISSORS, CUT 4 SECTIONS HALFWAY DOWN.

FLUFF IT UP!

PULL UP THE INNERMOST SECTIONS AND IT WILL SLIDE UP INTO A PAPER TREE.

The Paper Tower

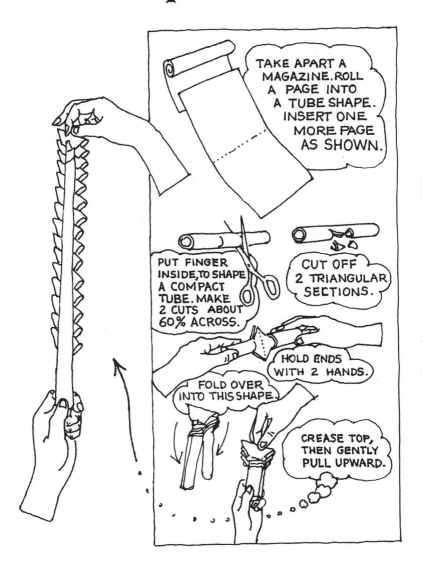

A Dollar Bill Ring

①

FOLD OVER THE TOP MARGIN OF AN UNWRINKLED DOLLAR.

② FOLD AGAIN AS SHOWN, SO THAT THE **ONE** IS CENTERED BETWEEN THE TOP AND THE FOLD.

THE **ONE** WILL BECOME THE SIGNET OF THE RING.

③ FOLD DOWN TOP EDGE TO MEET THE FOLDED EDGE.

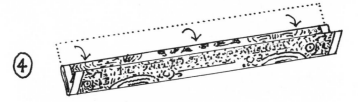

④

PULL UP THE ONE SECTION TO VERTICAL POSITION,
THEN FOLD OVER UPPER SECTION, ONE MORE TIME.
FOLD DOWN THE ONE SECTION SO THAT YOU HAVE
A FLAT BAND.

⑤

MAKE A RIGHT ANGLE FOLD AT THE LETTER "D" IN UNITED.

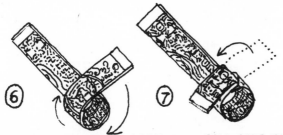

⑥ LOOP THE LONG END AROUND
TO FORM RING.

⑦ FOLD OVER TO MAKE
A CREASE FOR SIGNET.

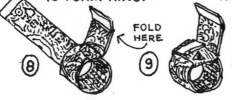

FOLD
HERE

⑧ RAISE SIGNET AGAIN
WRAP LONG PIECE COMPLETELY
AROUND THE RING SHAPE.

⑨

⑩ TUCK END TAB
UNDER FOLDS TO
COMPLETE THE RING.

Make A Decorative Paper Box

FIND A REPRODUCTION
OF A PICTURE YOU LIKE
AND MAKE IT SQUARE.

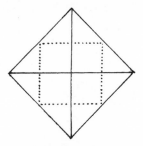

TURN IT OVER. MARK
STRAIGHT LINES TO
CORNERS. DOTTED LINES
ARE FOR NEXT FOLD.

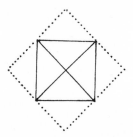

FOLD ALL 4 CORNERS
TO CENTER POINT.

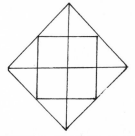

UNFOLD BACK TO FLAT
SHAPE, SO THAT THE
CREASES CAN BE USED
IN NEXT STEP.

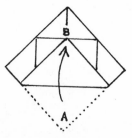

FOLD UP CORNER A
TO CREASE B THEN
UNFOLD BACK FLAT.

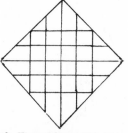

DO THE SAME TO ALL 4
CORNERS, SO THAT THE
FOLD/CREASES LOOK LIKE THIS.

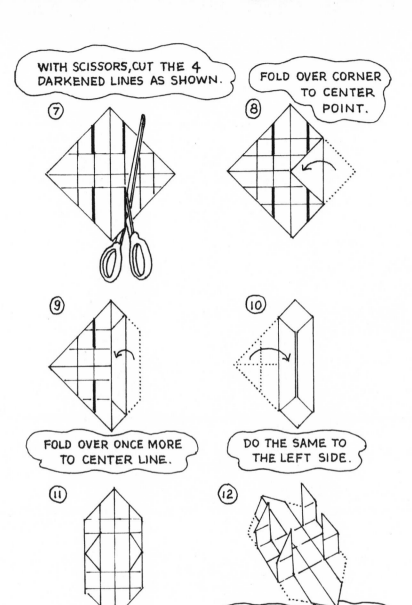

WITH SCISSORS, CUT THE 4 DARKENED LINES AS SHOWN.

⑦

FOLD OVER CORNER TO CENTER POINT.

⑧

⑨

FOLD OVER ONCE MORE TO CENTER LINE.

⑩

DO THE SAME TO THE LEFT SIDE.

⑪

UNFOLD BACK TO THIS SHAPE.

⑫

THIS 3D DRAWING SHOWS HOW THE 4 FLAPS ARE RAISED VERTICALLY.

43

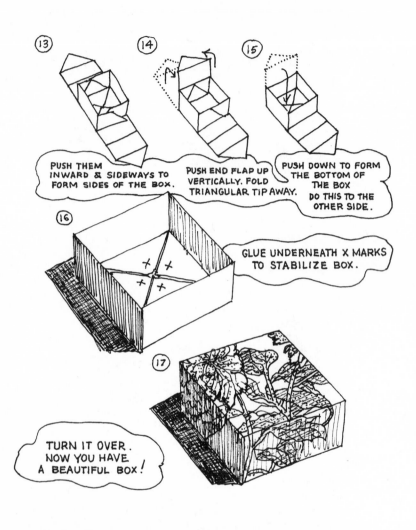

(13) PUSH THEM INWARD & SIDEWAYS TO FORM SIDES OF THE BOX.

(14) PUSH END FLAP UP VERTICALLY. FOLD TRIANGULAR TIP AWAY.

(15) PUSH DOWN TO FORM THE BOTTOM OF THE BOX DO THIS TO THE OTHER SIDE.

(16) GLUE UNDERNEATH X MARKS TO STABILIZE BOX.

(17) TURN IT OVER. NOW YOU HAVE A BEAUTIFUL BOX!

TO MAKE A COMPLETLY ENCLOSED BOX, REPEAT ALL
PROCEDURES, BUT MEASURE SQUARED PAPER ¼"LESS.
THIS CAN BE THE BOTTOM OF A COMPLETELY ENCLOSED BOX.

Pick Up An Egg Yolk

SOMETHING THAT ARTISTS DO TO PAINT WITH EGG TEMPERA

CRACK OPEN AN EGG.

SEPARATE THE EGG WHITE...

FROM THE YOLK.

PLACE THE YOLK ON THE PALM OF ONE HAND.

NOW BEGIN A PROCESS THAT REMOVES THE EXCESS EGG WHITE FROM THE YOLK SAC... DONE BY MOVING THE YOLK, BACK & FORTH, FROM PALM TO PALM.

WITH EACH TRANSFER, WIPE THE MOISTURE FROM FREE HAND ON A TOWEL.

NOW, GENTLY & CAREFULLY PICK UP THE YOLK.

THE ARTIST THEN POKES A HOLE THROUGH THE SAC AND COLLECTS THE PURE YOLK, TO BE MIXED WITH PIGMENT & WATER.

Dollar Bill Bow Tie

① FOLD DOLLAR BILL IN HALF AS SHOWN. THEN UNFOLD.

② TURN OVER FACE DOWN.
   FOLD TOP EDGE TO MIDDLE.

③ REPEAT ON OPPOSITE HALF.

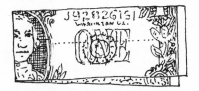

④ FOLD IN HALF AS SHOWN.

BURNISH ALL FOLDED EDGES WITH YOUR FINGERNAIL.

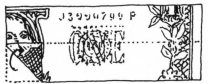

⑤ FOLD CORNER UP TO MIDDLE CREASE.

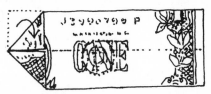

⑥ DO THE SAME TO TOP CORNER.

⑦ FOLD THE SAME CORNERS INTO OPPOSITE DIRECTION

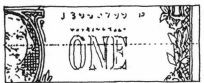

⑧ CREASE, THEN UNFOLD AGAIN.

⑨ NOW PUSH IN BOTH TRIANGLES...

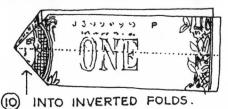

⑩ INTO INVERTED FOLDS.

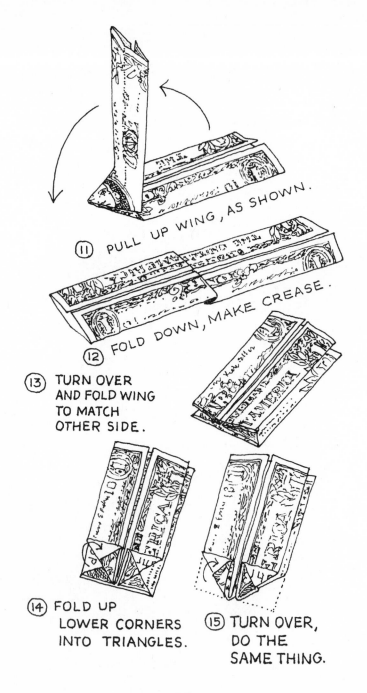

⑪ PULL UP WING, AS SHOWN.

⑫ FOLD DOWN, MAKE CREASE.

⑬ TURN OVER
AND FOLD WING
TO MATCH
OTHER SIDE.

⑭ FOLD UP
LOWER CORNERS
INTO TRIANGLES.

⑮ TURN OVER,
DO THE
SAME THING.

48

NOW THE FUN PART!

PUT THUMBS IN FRONT
AND FOREFINGERS BEHIND
GEORGE'S FACE, WHILE GENTLY
PRESSING THE FOLDS
INTO A FLAT SQUARE SHAPE.

AND HERE IT IS!

The Match Head Bottle Imp

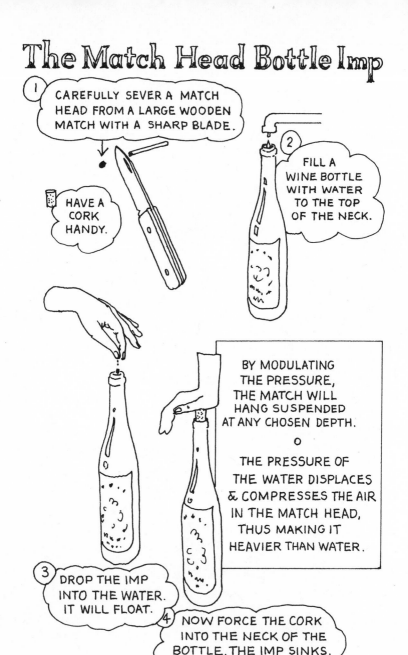

1. CAREFULLY SEVER A MATCH HEAD FROM A LARGE WOODEN MATCH WITH A SHARP BLADE.

HAVE A CORK HANDY.

2. FILL A WINE BOTTLE WITH WATER TO THE TOP OF THE NECK.

BY MODULATING THE PRESSURE, THE MATCH WILL HANG SUSPENDED AT ANY CHOSEN DEPTH.

o

THE PRESSURE OF THE WATER DISPLACES & COMPRESSES THE AIR IN THE MATCH HEAD, THUS MAKING IT HEAVIER THAN WATER.

3. DROP THE IMP INTO THE WATER. IT WILL FLOAT.

4. NOW FORCE THE CORK INTO THE NECK OF THE BOTTLE. THE IMP SINKS. HOW COME?

Have Some Tricks of Your Own?

SEND US YOUR FAVORITE TRICK; WE'LL POST THE BEST
ON OUR WEBSITE (WWW.SHELTERPUB.COM).
SEND THEM TO TRICKS@SHELTERPUB.COM
OR FAX TO 415-868-9053.

About the Author

ARTHUR OKAMURA IS PROFESSOR EMERITUS AT THE CALIFORNIA COLLEGE OF ARTS AND CRAFTS, WHERE HE TAUGHT FOR OVER THIRTY YEARS. HIS WORK IS IN THE PERMANENT COLLECTIONS AT THE CORCORAN GALLERY, THE SMITHSONIAN INSTITUTION, AND THE NATIONAL GALLERY OF ART IN WASHINGTON, D.C., THE WHITNEY MUSEUM OF AMERICAN ART IN NEW YORK, THE SAN FRANCISCO MUSEUM OF MODERN ART, AND NUMEROUS OTHER MAJOR VENUES. ARTHUR WORKS IN ALL KINDS OF MEDIA: PAINTING, DRAWING, PHOTOGRAPHY, SCULPTURE, COMPUTER GRAPHICS, AND SILKSCREEN. HE HAS CO-AUTHORED SEVERAL BOOKS, ONE WITH POET ROBERT CREELEY, TITLED *1, 2, 3, 4, 5, 6, 7, 8, 9, 0*. A FEW YEARS AGO HE MADE SOME 200 BRIGHTLY COLORED TROPICAL FISH OUT OF PAPER MACHE. RECENTLY HE DID A SERIES OF PAINTINGS ON A MACINTOSH G4 COMPUTER. HIS LATEST PROJECT IS A SERIES OF OIL PAINTINGS ON CANVAS BASED ON PHOTOS HE TAKES WITH A NIKON COOLPIX 950 DIGITAL CAMERA. HE ALSO CARVES ON ROCKS, BUILDS SHIMMERING SHALLOW-DISH POOLS FOR HIS GARDEN, AND PERFORMS THE TRICKS IN THIS BOOK TO THE DELIGHT OF FRIENDS AND STRANGERS.

Credits

EDITOR: LLOYD KAHN

PRODUCTION MANAGER: RICK GORDON

GRAPHICS PRODUCTION: ROBERT LEWANDOWSKI

DESIGN TUNEUP: DAVID WILLS

COVER DESIGN HELP: LESLEY KAHN

COPYWRITING AND CONSULTATION: GEORGE YOUNG

PHOTO OF ARTHUR: JOHN DOSS

PROOFREADING: FRANCES BOWLES

PRODUCTION HARDWARE

APPLE MACINTOSH G3/400, POWER COMPUTING POWERCENTER PRO 210, AGFA ARCUS II SCANNER, GCC ELITE XL 20/600 LASER PRINTER, EPSON STYLUS COLOR 3000 PRINTER

PRODUCTION SOFTWARE

QUARKXPRESS, ADOBE PHOTOSHOP, MICROSOFT WORD

TYPEFACE (FOR TYPESET PAGES OF BOOK)

OKAMURA SANS SERIF AND OKAMURA DISPLAY TYPE
FONTS CREATED BY ALEXANDER WALTER, MIDDLETOWN, NJ

PRINTING

MALLOY LITHOGRAPHING, INC., ANN ARBOR, MICHIGAN, U.S.A.

PAPER

60 LB. GLATFELTER OFF-WHITE ANTIQUE
ACIDPFREE, 85 PERCENT RECYCLED (10 PERCENT POST-CONSUMER)